VERSE

Chosen by Jennifer Curry

Illustrated by Graham Thompson

Beaver Books

Dedication
This book is for Henry and Sophie,
with love

A Beaver Original

Published by Arrow Books Limited
17-21 Conway Street, London W1P 6JD

A division of the Hutchinson Publishing Group

London Melbourne Sydney Auckland
Johannesburg and agencies throughout
the world

First published in 1981
Fifth impression 1985

Set in Bembo

Printed and bound in Great Britain by
Anchor Brendon Limited, Tiptree, Essex

ISBN 0 09 944230 2

Contents

Author's Acknowledgements

Very many people have helped me to gather together the poems in this book – a lot of friends, teachers, parents and children, especially children. I would like to thank them all, but particularly, my assistant, *Graeme Curry*, for his imagination, hard work and everlasting fund of good ideas; and also *June Shirfield* and the children in her class at Downton Primary School; *Greta Pike*; *Sandy Mason*; the *Salisbury Times and Journal*; *St Edmund's Arts Centre Writers' Workshop*; *the Director, Wiltshire Library and Museum Service*; *the library of ILEA's Centre for Language in Primary Education*; and the many *Beaver Bulletin Readers* who sent in their favourite school rhymes.

Juniper Curry

Our School

I go to Weld Park Primary,
It's near the Underpass
And five blocks past the Cemetery
And two roads past the Gas
Works with the big tower that smells so bad
   me and me mates put our hankies over our
     faces and pretend we're being attacked
       by poison gas . . . and that.

There's this playground with lines for rounders,
And cricket stumps chalked on the wall,
And kids with their coats for goalposts
Booting a tennis ball
Around all over the place and shoutin' and arguin'
   about offside and they always kick it over
     the garden wall next door and she
       goes potty and tells our head teacher
        and he gets right ratty with
         everybody and stops us playin'
          football . . .
            . . . and everything.

We have this rule at our school
You've to wait till the whistle blows
And you can't go in till you hear it
Not even if it snows
And your wellies get filled with water and your socks
   go all soggy and start slipping down your legs
     and your hands get so cold they go all
       crumpled and you can't undo
        the buttons of your mac when
         you do get inside . . .
          . . . it's true.

The best thing is our classroom.
When it's fine you can see right far,
Past the Catholic Cathedral
Right to the Morris Car
Works where me Dad works as a fitter and sets off
    right early every morning in these overalls
        with his snap in this sandwich box and
            a flask of tea and always moanin'
                about the money . . . honest.

In Hall we pray for brotherly love
And sing hymns that are ever so long
And the Head shouts at Linda Nutter
Who's always doing wrong.
She can't keep out of trouble because
    she's always talkin'
        she can't stop our teacher says she
            must have been injected with
                a gramophone needle she talks
                    so much and
that made me laugh once
not any more though I've heard it
    too often . . . teachers!

Loving your enemy sounds all right
Until you open your eyes
And you're standing next to Nolan
Who's always telling lies
About me and getting me into trouble and about
   three times a week I fight him after school
     it's like a habit I've got
       but I can't love him even though
         I screw my eyes up real hard and try like
         mad, but if it wasn't him it
          would be somebody else
          I mean
          you've got to have enemies . . .
          . . . haven't you?

We sing 'O to be a pilgrim'
And think about God and heaven
And then we're told the football team lost
By thirteen goals to seven
But that's not bad because St Xavier's don't half have
   big lads in their team and last time we played
     they beat us eighteen one and this time
       we got seven goals . . .
         . . . didn't we?

Then we have our lessons,
We have Science and English and Maths,
Except on Wednesday morning
When our class goes to the baths
And it's not half cold and Peter Bradberry's
    fingers went all wrinkled and blue last week
        and I said, 'You're goin' to die, man'
            but he pushed me under the water and I had to
            hold my breath for fifteen minutes.
                But he's still alive though . . .
                    . . . he is.

Friday's my favourite day though,
We have Art all afternoon
And I never care what happens
'Cos I know it's home-time soon
And I'm free for two whole days but I think
    sometimes it wouldn't be half so good
        having this weekend if we didn't have five
            days
                of
                    school
                        in
                            between—
Would it?

Gareth Owen

8

GOING TO SCHOOL

Meet-on-the-Road

'Now, pray, where are you going?' said
                            Meet-on-the-Road.
'To school, sir, to school, sir,' said
                            Child-as-it-Stood.

'What have you in your basket, child?' said
                            Meet-on-the-Road.
'My dinner, sir, my dinner, sir,' said
                            Child-as-it-Stood.

'What have you for dinner, child?' said
                            Meet-on-the-Road.
'Some pudding, sir, some pudding, sir,' said
                            Child-as-it-Stood.

'Oh, then, I pray, give me a share,' said
                            Meet-on-the-Road.
'I've little enough for myself, sir,' said
                            Child-as-it-Stood.

'What have you got that cloak on for?' said
                            Meet-on-the-Road.
'To keep the wind and cold from me,' said
                            Child-as-it-Stood.

'I wish the wind would blow through you,' said
                            Meet-on-the-Road.
'Oh, what a wish! What a wish!' said
                            Child-as-it-Stood.

'Pray, what are those bells ringing for?' said
                              Meet-on-the-Road.
'To ring bad spirits home again,' said
                              Child-as-it-Stood.

'Oh, then I must be going, child!' said
                              Meet-on-the-Road.
'So fare you well, so fare you well,' said
                              Child-as-it-Stood.

Anon

Going to School in the Country

A long walk,
two miles or more,
up hill and down, before
I get to the school gate;
I do not stop and talk
to anyone on the way,
and I am never late.
At eight o'clock today
I passed by Gunter's farm,
the men were making hay,
and then I met a herd of cows
lumbering along;
they meant no harm,
and over the fields where Gunter ploughs
each spring, a lark rose up in song;
at the end of the tall-hedged lane,
two cottages and a rick,
and there I peeled a hazel stick;
at half past nine was there,
beating a shower of rain,
ready for Miss Jones and morning prayer.

Leonard Clark

Going to School in Town

A long walk,
half a mile or more,
over four noisy roads, before
I reach the high school wall,
covered with pictures in chalk,
and hear the playground bell call
us into our lines.
I go past twenty shops, a shellfish stall,
and through a smelly tunnel where
the sun never shines,
and then across the square,
around a corner by the old King's Head
and there must wait,
do what my teacher said,
for the green light to say
that I can cross the road;
bus after bus every day
and lorries each with a different load.
And then I am
dodging the factory where they make jam,
and at last run into school there,
ready for Mr Smith and morning prayer.

Leonard Clark

The Lollipop Lady

The Lollipop Lady is not
as tall as the lollipop
but she shines in the wet.
Some days I forget
about her, and stop
with a skid in a puddle
and there is her red and white bubble
all of a sudden, twice.
The Lollipop Lady is nice;
she sorts out the muddle
and holds my hand
and stops the cars with her magic wand
so I can walk, where there aren't any stripes,
past huge big lorries and motor bikes
which roar and shake and
smoke like dragons; but all of them wait
for the Lollipop Lady's wave –
for the children. When she
smiles and nods at me
I can cross the road. If I'm as brave
as her when I grow up, *I* could be
a shining Lollipop Lady.

Jane Whittle

Marbles in my Pocket

Marbles in my pocket!
Winter-time's begun!
Marbles in my pocket
That rattle when I run!

Heavy in my pocket
On the way to school;
Smooth against my fingers,
Round and hard and cool;

Marbles in my pocket,
Blue and green and red,
And some are yellow-golden,
And some are brown instead.

Marbles in the playground,
Big and little ring –
Oh, I like playing marbles,
But that's a different thing.

Marbles in my pocket,
Smooth within my hand,
That's the part that's nicest;
Do you understand?

Marbles in my pocket
To rattle when I run!
For winter days are here again,
And marble-time's begun!

Lydia Pender

I've Got an Apple Ready

My hair's tightly plaited;
I've a bright blue bow;
I don't want my breakfast,
And now I must go.

My satchel's on my shoulder;
Nothing's out of place;
And I've got an apple ready,
Just in case.

So it's 'Goodbye, Mother!'
And off down the street!
Briskly at first
On pit-a-pat feet,

But slow and more slow
As I reach the tarred
Trackway that runs
By Hodson's Yard;

For it's there sometimes
Bill Craddock waits for me
To snatch off my beret
And throw it in a tree.

Bill Craddock is leaning
On Hodson's rails;
Bill with thin hands
And dirty nails;

Bill with a front tooth
Broken and bad;
His dark eyes cruel,
And somewhat sad.

Often there are workmen,
And then he doesn't dare;
But this morning I feel
He'll be there.

At the corner he will pounce . . .
But quickly I'll say
'Hallo, Bill, have an apple!' –
In an ordinary way.

I'll push it in his hand
And walk right on;
And when I'm round the corner
I'll run.

John Walsh

Bus to School

Rounding a corner
It comes to stay.
Quick. Grab the rail!
Now we're off on our way . . .

Here in the bus though
There's plenty to see:
Boys full of talk about
Last night's T.V.
Girls with their violins,
Armfuls of twigs
And flowers for the teacher.
Bartlett and Biggs
Conductor who chats with them,
Jokes about cricket;
Machine that flicks out
A white ribbon of ticket . . .

Conductor now waiting,
Firm as a rock,
For Billy, whose penny's
Slid down his sock,
Conductor frowning,
With finger on handle:
Poor Billy blushes,
Undoes his sandal . . .
'Hold very tight, please!
Any more fares?'
Whistling conductor
Goes clumping upstairs . . .

Boots up above, now!
Boys coming down! . . .
Over the hump bridge
And into the town.

John Walsh

The School Bus Breaks Down

As up the hill the school bus goes,
Just listen how it puffs and blows.
It coughs and splutters as it tries
To drag its body up the rise,
Until at last it wearies out
And stops. Then with a joyful shout
The children jump down to the ground
And laugh and skip and run around.

'We'll all be late for school! Hurray!
It's not our fault!' they chant with glee.
'Sit down. We'll soon be on our way!'
The driver roars. 'Don't crowd round me!'

He takes a crank, and twirls it round.
The boys and girls soon hear the sound
Of engines turning. In they hop.
And with another start and stop
The bus moves off. With downcast face
Each child sits in his normal place.
'School after all!' they sadly say.
'I thought we might have missed today!'

Phyllis Telfer and Hermea Goodman

The Schoolboy

I love to rise in a summer morn
When the birds sing on every tree;
The distant huntsman winds his horn,
And the sky-lark sings with me.
O! what sweet company.

But to go to school in a summer morn,
O! it drives all joy away;
Under a cruel eye outworn,
The little ones spend the day
In sighing and dismay.

Ah! then at times I drooping sit,
And spend many an anxious hour,
Nor in my book can I take delight,
Nor sit in learning's bower,
Worn thro' with the dreary shower.

How can the bird that is born for joy
Sit in a cage and sing?
How can a child, when fears annoy,
But droop his tender wing,
And forget his youthful spring?

William Blake

First Day at School

A millionbillionwillion miles from home
Waiting for the bell to go. (To go where?)
Why are they all so big, other children?
So noisy? So much at home they
must have been born in uniform.
Lived all their lives in playgrounds.
Spent the years inventing games
that don't let me in. Games
that are rough, that swallow you up.

And the railings.
All around, the railings.
Are they to keep out wolves and monsters?
Things that carry off and eat children?
Things you don't take sweets from?
Perhaps they're to stop us getting out
Running away from the lessins. Lessin.
What does a lessin look like?
Sounds small and slimy.
They keep them in glassrooms.
Whole rooms made out of glass. Imagine.

I wish I could remember my name
Mummy said it would come in useful.
Like wellies. When there's puddles.
Yellowwellies. I wish she was here.
I think my name is sewn on somewhere
Perhaps the teacher will read it for me.
Tea'cher. The one who makes the tea.

Roger McGough

School Bell

Nine-o'Clock Bell!
Nine-o'Clock Bell!
All the small children and big ones as well,
Pulling their stockings up, snatching their hats,
Cheeking and grumbling and giving back-chats,
Laughing and quarrelling, dropping their things,
These at a snail's pace and those upon wings,
Lagging behind a bit, running ahead,
Waiting at corners for lights to turn red,
Some of them scurrying,
Others not worrying,
Carelessly trudging or anxiously hurrying,
All through the streets they are coming pell-mell
At the Nine-o'Clock
       Nine-o'Clock
       Nine-o'Clock
            Bell!

Eleanor Farjeon

The New Boy

Slowly he trundles into school clinging tightly to his
                            mother's hand,
Crying a little.
He holds his mother's dress shyly.
Children stand like giants to him when he is just a
                            scared mouse.
In the cloakroom the giants push around him
To reach their pegs.
He feels like a football.

Karen Aldous (aged 7)

IN THE CLASSROOM

In Hall

'All things bright and beautiful . . .'
How many late today?
There's mud all up the front staircase,
What is she going to say?

It's hot in here, I'm going to sneeze.
'All creatures great and small . . .'
A spider's dangling over her!
Where is it going to fall?

It might land softly in her hair –
would she feel it, d'you suppose?
Or, if it swung a little bit,
it might settle on her nose.

'All things wise and wonderful . . .'
The teachers stand in line.
It's only got an inch to go!
This may be a sign.

Oh, land on her, please land on her!
'The Lord God made them all . . .'
Then she'll forget she saw me there –
I was here, in Hall,

I wasn't late, I didn't leave
my footsteps on the stairs . . .
Oh! Spider, you must hurry up,
she's halfway through the prayers.

Spider, spider, burning bright . . .
'Three girls I want to see.
Where are you? You, and you, and . . . Oh!
What's this? Oh dear! Dear me! . . .'

A hundred eyes, eight hairy legs,
A shadow on the wall.
I wasn't there, I wasn't late.
The Lord God loves us all!

Jane Whittle

Morning Prayers

Late September, conker time,
Back at school the children file
Into the assembly hall.
Smells of freshly polished floors,
Disinfectants, sunlight soap,
Familiar sounds and smells will long
Recall those early days of school.
The day begins with morning prayers.

Headmaster strides into the hall,
Crowlike in black flapping gown,
And as the clock is striking nine,
He calls out, 'Silence please.'
And prayers begin.
The youngsters, like automatons
Repeat the words in all the same
Uncomprehending monotones,
'Ah Father wishart in Heaven,
Harold be thy name. . . .'

E. Graham Yooll

Profile of a Desk

Lots of things are on this desk,
John is this and Fred is that
Pete's a burk and Harry too,
Little hearts saying 'I love you',
Teachers are gits – John loves Mary,
Peter Houseman is a fairy.

J. C. Jeffery

I Went Back

I went back after a cold
And nothing was the same.
When the register was called
Even my name
Sounded queer . . . new . . .
(And I was born here too!)
Everyone knew more than me,
Even Kenneth Hannaky
Who's worst usually.
They'd made a play
And puppets from clay
While I was away,
Learnt a song about Cape Horn,
Five guinea pigs were born.
Daffodils in the blue pot,
(I planted them)
Bloomed, and I was not
There to see.
Jean had a new coat
And someone, probably George,
Smashed my paper boat.
Monday was a dreadful day.
I wished I was still away.
Tuesday's news day.
I took my stamps to show,
Made a clown called Jo,
Learnt that song from John . . .
Cold's almost gone . . .
And . . . the smallest guinea pig,
Silky black and brown thing,
I'm having
Till spring.

Gwen Dunn

From the Classroom Window

Sometimes, when heads are deep in books,
And nothing stirs,
The sunlight touches that far hill,
And its three dark firs;
Then on those trees I fix my eyes –
And teacher hers.

Together awhile we contemplate
The air-blue sky
And those dark tree-tops; till, with a tiny
Start and sigh,
She turns again to the printed page –
And so do I.

But our two thoughts have met out there
Where no school is –
Where, among call of birds and faint
Shimmer of bees,
They rise in sunlight, resinous, warm –
Those dark fir-trees.

John Walsh

From the classroom window.

From the classroom window.
I can see trees looking like bands of
black lace.
The fringe of grass protecting the
frightened fence like tall thin body
guards.
The small sparrows black birds and
magpies looking like little midget
witches swooping down on their broom
sticks to get some food.

Neil Bartlett (aged 8)

Timothy Winters

Timothy Winters comes to school
With eyes as wide as a football—pool,
Ears like bombs and teeth like splinters:
A blitz of a boy is Timothy Winters.

His belly is white, his neck is dark,
And his hair is an exclamation-mark.
His clothes are enough to scare a crow
And through his britches the blue winds blow.

When teacher talks he won't hear a word
And he shoots down dead the arithmetic-bird,
He licks the patterns off his plate
And he's not even heard of the Welfare State.

Timothy Winters has bloody feet
And he lives in a house on Suez Street,
He sleeps in a sack on the kitchen floor
And they say there aren't boys like him any more.

Old Man Winters likes his beer
And his missus ran off with a bombardier,
Grandma sits in the grate with a gin
And Timothy's dosed with an aspirin.

The Welfare Worker lies awake
But the law's as tricky as a ten-foot snake,
So Timothy Winters drinks his cup,
And slowly goes on growing up.

At Morning Prayers the Master helves
For children less fortunate than ourselves,
And the loudest response in the room is when
Timothy Winters roars 'Amen!'

So come one angel, come on ten:
Timothy Winters says 'Amen
Amen amen amen amen,'
Timothy Winters, Lord.
                    Amen.

Charles Causley

Against Idleness and Mischief

How doth the little busy bee
　　Improve each shining hour,
And gather honey all the day
　　From every opening flower!

How skilfully she builds her cell!
　　How neat she spreads the wax!
And labours hard to store it well
　　With the sweet food she makes.

In works of labour or of skill
　　I would be busy too;
For Satan finds some mischief still
　　For idle hands to do.

In books, or work, or healthful play,
　　Let my first years be passed,
That I may give for every day
　　Some good account at last.

Isaac Watts

God Made the Bees

God made the bees,
The bees make the honey,
We do all the dirty work,
The teachers make the money.

Sent in by Lisa Adlard

Build a bonfire
Build a bonfire
Put the teacher at the top
Put headmaster in the middle
And burn the blooming lot.

Sent in by
Josephine Powney (aged 12)

Pounds, shillings, pence,
Teacher has no sense,
She came to school
To act the fool,
Pounds, shillings, pence.

Sir is kind and sir is gentle,
Sir is strong and sir is mental.

Land of soapy water,
Teacher's having a bath,
Headmaster's looking through the keyhole,
Having a jolly good laugh.

Sent in by Jane Whitfield

I had a dream last night,
A dream that made me laugh,
I dreamt I was a piece of soap,
In our headmistress's bath!

Sent in by Jackie Watts (aged 10)

My Teacher

Mrs Bond is nice she shouts
and makes me jump
and when she says get
your sum books out I
nearly faint and when she
says put on your pumps I
think I run round the world
and I run across the playground
and when she says run I run and when
she says jump I jump

Kevin Brown (aged 6)

Rodge Said

Rodge said,
'Teachers – they want it all ways –
You're jumping up and down on a chair
or something
and they grab hold of you and say
"Would you do that sort of thing in your own
home?"

'So you say, "No."
And they say,
"Well don't do it here then,"

'But if you say, "Yes, I do it at home."
they say,
"Well, we don't want that sort of thing
going on here
thank you very much."

'Teachers – they get you all ways,'
Rodge said.

Michael Rosen

Teacher's Pet

In the class there is usually a teacher's pet
Who is so goody goody.
Every class has one, no fret.
The girls are extra special teachers' pets (creeps!)
Teachers' pets do anything for the teachers –
'Yes, miss! No, miss! O.K. miss.
Anything you say, miss.'

Philip Moody (aged 9)

The Description of a Good Boy

The boy that is good,
Does learn his book well;
And if he can't read,
Will strive for to spell.

His school he does love,
And when he is there,
For play and for toys,
No time can he spare.

His mind is full bent,
On what he is taught;
He sits in the school,
As one full of thought.

Though not as a mope,
Who quakes out of fear
The whip or the rod
Should fall on his rear.

But like a good lad
Who aims to be wise,
He thinks on his book,
And not on his toys.

His mien will be grave,
Yet, if you would know,
He plays with an air,
When a dunce dare not so.

His aim is to learn,
His task is his play;
And when he has learned,
He smiles and looks gay.

Henry Dixon

The Lesson

Chaos ruled OK in the classroom
as bravely the teacher walked in
the havocwreakers ignored him
his voice was lost in the din

'The theme for today is violence
and homework will be set
I'm going to teach you a lesson
one that you'll never forget'

He picked on a boy who was shouting
and throttled him then and there
then garrotted the girl behind him
(the one with the grotty hair)

Then sword in hand he hacked his way
between the chattering rows
'First come, first severed,' he declared
'fingers, feet, or toes'

He threw the sword at a latecomer
it struck with deadly aim
then pulling out a shotgun
he continued with his game

The first blast cleared the backrow
(where those who skive hang out)
they collapsed like rubber dinghies
when the plug's pulled out

'Please may I leave the room sir?'
a trembling vandal enquired
'Of course you may' said teacher
put the gun to his temple and fired

The Head popped a head round the doorway
to see why a din was being made
nodded understandingly
then tossed in a grenade

And when the ammo was well spent
with blood on every chair
Silence shuffled forward
with its hands up in the air.

The teacher surveyed the carnage
the dying and the dead
He waggled a finger severely
'Now let that be a lesson' he said.

Roger McGough

There was an old man who said, 'Do
Tell me *how* I should add two and two?
    I think more and more
     That it makes about four –
But I fear that is almost too few.'

Anon

Maths Problems

Please add these up:
One ton of sawdust.
One ton of old newspaper.
Four tons of string.
One half-ton of fat.
Have you got all that in your head?
'Yes.'
I thought so.

Take any number.
Add ten.
Subtract three.
Now close your eyes.
(Your friend closes his eyes.)
Dark, isn't it!

Alvin Schwartz

Maths Lesson Rules

Always subtract bottom from top.
A plus and a plus equals a minus
or, a plus depending on the month
equals circumference but
equals fruit and pastry depending on the lesson.
Don't blow bubbles.
Remember to write who you love on desks
Don't eat the chalk
Come to lessons.
Don't sit on chairs – sit on the floor (it's safer).
Enter cupboards at your own risk.
Try to avoid flirting with new maths books.
Skive when possible. Don't get caught.
Look interested – in what's going on outside.
Cheat in exams.
Don't scribble rude words on the board
write them clearly.
Never go to detentions, or other dishonourable
                                    functions.
Don't pluck your eyebrows – save that for
                                    geography.

Christine Bates and Jill Etheridge

Exercise Book

Two and two four
four and four eight
eight and eight sixteen . . .
Once again! says the master
Two and two four
four and four eight
eight and eight sixteen.
But look! the lyre-bird
high on the wing
the child sees it
the child hears it
the child calls it.
Save me
play with me
bird!
So the bird alights
and plays with the child
Two and two four . . .
Once again! says the master
and the child plays
and the bird plays too . . .
Four and four eight
eight and eight sixteen
and twice sixteen makes what?
Twice sixteen makes nothing
least of all thirty-two
anyhow
and off they go.

For the child has hidden
the bird in his desk
and all the children
hear its song
and all the children
hear the music
and eight and eight in their turn
off they go
and four and four and two and two
in their turn fade away
and one and one make neither one nor two
but one by one off they go.
And the lyre-bird sings
and the child sings
and the master shouts
When you've quite finished playing the fool!
But all the children
are listening to the music
and the walls of the classroom
quietly crumble.
The windowpanes turn
once more to sand
the ink is sea
the desk is trees
the chalk is cliffs
and the quill pen
a bird again.

Jaques Prévert (translated by Paul Dehn)

Tingle-tangle Titmouse

Come hither, little piggy-wig,
Come and learn your letters,
And you shall have a knife and fork
To eat with, like your betters.
'Oh no,' the little pig replied,
'My trough will do as well;
I'd rather eat my victuals there
Than learn to read and spell.'

     With a tingle-tangle titmouse,
     Robin knows great A,
     B and C and D and E,
     F,G,H,I,J,K.

Come hither, little pussy-cat;
If you will grammar study,
I'll give you silver clogs to wear
Whene'er the weather's muddy.
'Oh, if I grammar learn,' said Puss,
'Your house will in a trice
Be overrun from top to bottom
With the rats and mice.'

    Chorus

Come hither, little puppy-dog;
I'll give you a new collar
If you will learn to read and spell
And be a clever scholar.
'Oh no,' the little dog replied,
'I've other fish to fry,
For I must learn to guard the house
And bark when thieves are nigh.'

    Chorus

Come hither then, good little boy,
And learn your alphabet,
And you a pair of boots and spurs
Like your papa shall get.
'Oh yes, I'll learn my alphabet;
And when I well can read,
My kind papa has promised me
A little long-tailed steed.'

With a tingle-tangle titmouse,
Robin knows great A,
B and C and D and E,
F,G,H,I,J,K.

Traditional

The ABC

'Twas midnight in the schoolroom
And every desk was shut,
When suddenly from the alphabet
Was heard a loud 'Tut-tut!'

Said A to B, 'I don't like C;
His manners are a lack.
For all I ever see of C
Is a semicircular back!'

'I disagree,' said D to B,
'I've never found C so.
From where *I* stand, he seems to be
An uncompleted O.'

C was vexed. 'I'm much perplexed,
You criticise my shape.
I'm made like that, to help spell Cat
And Cow and Cool and Cape.'

'He's right,' said E; said F, 'Whoopee!'
Said G, "Ip, 'ip, 'ooray!'
'You're dropping me,' roared H to G.
'Don't do it please, I pray!'

'Out of my way,' LL said to K.
'I'll make poor I look Ill.'
To stop this stunt, J stood in front,
And presto! ILL was JILL.

'U know,' said V, 'that W
Is twice the age of me,
For as a Roman V is five
I'm half as young as he.'

X and Y yawned sleepily,
'Look at the time!' they said.
They all jumped in to beddy byes
And the last one in was Z!

Spike Milligan

Punctuation Puzzle

Caesar entered on his head
A helmet on each foot
A sandal in his hand he had
His trusty sword to boot.

BANANANANANANANANA

I thought I'd win the spelling bee
    And get right to the top,
But I started to spell 'banana,'
    And I didn't know when to stop.

William Cole

A was an Archer

A was an Archer, and shot at a frog,
B was a Blindman, and led by a dog.
C was a Cutpurse, and lived in disgrace,
D was a Drunkard, and had a red face.
E was an Eater, a glutton was he,
F was a Fighter, and fought with a flea.
G was a Giant, and pulled down a house,
H was a Hunter, and hunted a mouse.
I was an Ill man, and hated by all,
K was a Knave, and he robbed great and small.
L was a Liar, and told many lies,
M was a Madman, and beat out his eyes.
N was a Nobleman, nobly born,
O was an Ostler, and stole horses' corn.
P was a Pedlar, and sold many pins,
Q was a Quarreller, and broke both his shins.
R was a Rogue, and ran about town,
S was a Sailor, a man of renown.
T was a Tailor, and knavishly bent,
U was a Usurer, took ten per cent.
W was a Writer, and money he earned,
X was one Xenophon, prudent and learn'd.
Y was a Yeoman, and worked for his bread,
Z was one Zeno the Great, but he's dead.

Anon (1700)

A Good Poem

I like a good poem
one with lots of fighting
in it. Blood and the
clanging of armour. Poems

against Scotland are good
and poems that defeat
the French with crossbows.
I don't like poems that

aren't about anything.
Sonnets are wet and
a waste of time.
Also poems that don't

know how to rhyme.
If I was a poem
I'd play football and
get picked for England.

Roger McGough

Poets

We had two poets come to our school
today
I liked them.
They read poems
And one even tried to sing.
They told us about poetry.
We had two poets come to our school
today.
I liked them.

Elaine Breden

The English Language

Some words have different meanings,
and yet they're spelt the same.
A cricket is an insect,
to play it – it's a game.
On every hand, in every land,
it's thoroughly agreed,
the English language to explain,
is very hard indeed.

Some **people** say that you're a dear,
yet dear is far from cheap.
A jumper is a thing you wear,
yet a jumper has to leap.
It's very clear, it's very queer,
and pray who is to blame
for different meanings to some words
pronounced and spelt the same?

A little journey is a trip,
a trip is when you fall.
It doesn't mean you have to dance
whene'er you hold a ball.
Now here's a thing that puzzles me:
musicians of good taste
will very often form a band –
I've one around my waist!

You spin a top, go for a spin,
or spin a yarn may be –
yet every spin's a different spin,
as you can plainly see.
Now here's a most peculiar thing,
'twas told me as a joke –
a dumb man wouldn't speak a word,
yet seized a wheel and spoke.

A door may often be ajar,
but give the door a slam,
and then your nerves receive a jar –
and then there's jars of jam.
You've heard, of course, of traffic jams,
and jams you give your thumbs.
And adders, too, one is a snake,
the other adds up sums.

A policeman is a copper,
it's a nickname (impolite!)
yet a copper in the kitchen
is an article you light.
On every hand, in every land,
it's thoroughly agreed –
the English language to explain
is very hard indeed!

Harry Hemsley

Latin is a language
As dead as dead can be,
First it killed the Romans
And now it's killing me.

The English Succession

The Norman Conquest all historians fix
To the year of Christ, one thousand sixty-six.
Two Wills, one Henry, Stephen, Kings are
                                    reckoned;
Then rose Plantagenet in Henry second.
First Richard, John, third Henry, Edwards three,
And second Richard in one line we see.
Fourth, fifth, and sixth Lancastrian Henrys reign;
Then Yorkist Edwards two, and Richard slain.
Next Tudor comes in seventh Henry's right,
Who the red rose engrafted on the white.
Eighth Henry, Edward sixth, first Mary, Bess;
Then Scottish Stuart's right the peers confess.
James, double Charles, a second James expelled;
With Mary, Will; then Anne the sceptre held.
Last, Brunswick's issue has two Georges given;
Late may the second pass from earth to heaven!

Anon (c. 1749)

Willy, Willy

Willy, Willy, Harry, Stee
Harry, Dick, John, Harry Three
One, Two, Three Neds, Richard Two
Henry Four, Five, Six, then who?
Neds Four, Five and Dick the Bad,
Harrys Twain and Ned the Lad.
Mary, Bessie, James the Vain
Charley, Charley, James again.
William and Mary, Anna Gloria
Four Georges, William, and Victoria.
Edward Seventh, and then –
George the Fifth in 1910!

Demeanour

Busy in study be thou, child,
And in the hall, meek and mild,
And at the table, merry and glad,
And at bed, soft and sad.

Anon (c. 1525)

The Dunce

Why does he still keep ticking?
  Why does his round white face
Stare at me over the books and ink,
  And mock at my disgrace?
Why does that thrush call, 'Dunce, dunce, dunce!'?
  Why does that bluebottle buzz?
Why does the sun so silent shine? –
  And what do I care if it does?

Walter de la Mare

Streemin

Im in the botom streme
Which meens Im not brigth
dont like reading
cant hardly write

but all these divishns
arnt reely fair
look at the cemtery
no streemin there

Roger McGough

Confusion

Jean get licks in school today
For hitting Janet Hill
It was just after recess time
And class was playful still
Janet pull Jean ribbon off
And throw it on the ground
Jean got vex and cuff Janet
Same time Miss turn around
Miss didn't ask no questions
She just start beating Jean
Tomorrow Jean mother coming
to fix-up Miss McLean

Odette Thomas

The Bully Asleep

This afternoon, when grassy
Scents through the classroom crept,
Bill Craddock laid his head
Down on his desk, and slept.

The children came round him:
Jimmy, Roger, and Jane;
They lifted his head timidly
And let it sink again.

'Look, he's gone sound asleep, Miss,'
Said Jimmy Adair;
'He stays up all night, you see;
His mother doesn't care.'

'Stand away from him children.'
Miss Andrews stooped to see.
'Yes, he's asleep; go on
With your writing, and let him be.'

'Now's a good chance!' whispered Jimmy,
And he snatched Bill's pen and hid it.
'Kick him under the desk, hard;
He won't know who did it.'

'Fill all his pockets with rubbish –
Paper, apple-cores, chalk.'
So they plotted, while Jane
Sat wide-eyed at their talk.

Not caring, not hearing,
Bill Craddock he slept on;
Lips parted, eyes closed –
Their cruelty gone.

'Stick him with pins!' muttered Roger.
'Ink down his neck!' said Jim.
But Jane, tearful and foolish,
Wanted to comfort him.

John Walsh

Nooligan

I'm a nooligan
don't give a toss
in our class
I'm the boss
(well, one of them)

I'm a nooligan
got a nard 'ead
step out of line
and youre dead
(well, bleedin)

I'm a nooligan
I spray me name
all over town
footballs me game
(well, watchin)

I'm a nooligan
violence is fun
gonna be a nassassin
or a nired gun
(well, a soldier)

Roger McGough

Upon Pagget

Pagget, a school-boy, got a sword, and then
He vowed destruction both to birch, and men:
Who would not think this yonker fierce to fight?
Yet coming home, but somewhat late, (last night)
'Untruss,' his master bade him; and that word
Made him take up his shirt, lay down his sword.

Robert Herrick

Deborah Delora

Deborah Delora, she liked a bit of fun –
She went to the baker's and bought a penny bun;
Dipped the bun in treacle and threw it at her teacher –
Deborah Delora! What a wicked creature!

The Toe Picker

She is tall and likes to show off
She picks her toe nails
That's why I can't stand her
She takes off her smelly socks and picks at her toes
She doesn't care what anyone says
She is the worst show off at school
She is slim and moves lightly
But still she picks her toes
Skin all gone
Nail all gone
It looks disgusting
Everyone tells her to stop it
But she still picks her toes
She is pretty and has a lot of friends
Just because I am her sister
She picks her toes in front of me
But she still picks her toes
HORRID, NASTY, HORRID.

Debbie Ward

The Marrog

My desk's at the back of the class
   And nobody, nobody knows
     I'm a Marrog from Mars
With a body of brass
     And seventeen fingers and toes.

Wouldn't they shriek if they knew
   I've three eyes at the back of my head
And my hair is bright purple
My nose is deep blue
   And my teeth are half-yellow, half-red

My five arms are silver, and spiked
   With knives on them sharper than spears.
I could go back right now, if I liked –
   And return in a million light-years.

I could gobble them all,
For I'm seven foot tall
And I'm breathing green flames from my ears.

Wouldn't they yell if they knew,
   If they guessed that a Marrog was here?
Ha-ha, they haven't a clue –
   Or wouldn't they tremble with fear!
'Look, look, a Marrog'
   They'd all scream – and SMACK
The blackboard would fall and the ceiling would
                    crack
   And teacher would faint, I suppose.
But I grin to myself, sitting right at the back
   And nobody, nobody knows.

R. C. Scriven

Scribbled on the Fly-leaves in Old School Books

Black is the raven
Black is the rook
But blacker the sinner
Who pinches this book.

This book is mine
This boot another
Touch not the one
For fear of the other.

He what takes what isn't his'n
When he's cotched, will go to prison.

Good News

The Board of Education has just set up new rules
That in the future they'll shut all the schools
On every April Fool's.

APRIL FOOL!
(Keep cool.)

William Cole

Board Rubber

Board rubber you're dusty
I bet you learn a lot
That concludes today's lesson.

Gina Staley

Last Lesson of the Day

Here we come,
Only to be trapped in,
For the agonising,
Moments of the day.
Through the door,
Down with the bag,
And up with the desk,
'Get that desk down,'
''Ere we go again.'
'Get out your work – quietly.'
The last moments lingered on,
Like a weary dog
Being pulled along by an impatient master.
Come on, the bell must ring,
Drrrrrrrinnnngggggggggggg!
Up with the desk,
In with the books,
Up with the bag
And out the door all as fast as
GREASE LIGHTENING.

Chris Palmer

SONGS

Mary had a little lamb,
    Its feet were black as soot,
And into Mary's bread and jam
    Its sooty foot it put.

Mary had a little lamb,
    It was a greedy glutton.
She fed it on ice-cream all day
    And now it's frozen mutton.

Mary had a little lamb,
    She ate it with mint sauce,
And everywhere that Mary went
    The lamb went too, of course.

Mary had a wristlet watch,
    She swallowed it one day,
And now she's taking Beecham's pills
    To pass the time away.

Mary had a little *cow*,
    It fed on safety pins;
And every time she milked the cow
    The milk came out in tins.

Never let your braces dangle,
Never let your braces dangle.
Poor old sport
He got caught
And went right through the mangle;
Went through the mangle he did, by gum,
Came out like linoleum,
Now he sings in kingdom-come:
Never let your braces dangle, chum.

I'm a knock-kneed chicken, I'm a bow-legged
sparrow,
Missed my bus so I went by barrow.
I went to the café for my dinner and my tea,
Too many radishes – Hick! Pardon me.

I went to the animal fair,
All the birds and the beasts were there,
The gay baboon by the light of the moon
Was combing his yellow hair.
The monkey fell from his bunk
And dropped on the elephant's trunk.
The elephant sneezed, and went down on his knees
And what became of the mon-key,
    mon-key, mon-key, mon-key,
    monk?

There was a bloomin' spider,
Climbed up a bloomin' spout,
Down came the rain
And washed the spider out.
Out came the sunshine
Dried up all the rain,
Up the bloomin' water spout
The blighter went again.

There's a long, long worm a-crawling
Across the roof of my tent.
I can hear the whistle calling,
And it's time I went.
There's the cold, cold water waiting
For me to take my morning dip.
And when I come back I'll find that worm
Upon my pillow-slip.

The Yellow Rose of Texas and the man from
                                    Laramie
Went down to Davy Crockett's to have a cup of tea;
The tea was so delicious, they had another cup,
And poor old Davy Crockett had to do the
                                    washing up.

After the ball was over
She lay on the sofa and sighed.
She put her false teeth in salt water
And took out her lovely glass eye.
She kicked her cork leg in the corner
And hung up her wig on the wall,
The rest of her went to bye-byes,
After the ball.

Mademoiselle from Armentières, parlez-vous,
She hasn't been kissed for forty years, parlez-vous.
The Prince of Wales was put in jail
For riding a horse without a tail,
Inky-pinky parlez-vous.

Jingle bells,
Batman smells,
Robin flew away,
Kojak lost his lollipop
And found it straight away.

Sent in by Jonathan David Riddell (aged 7)

Carols

'*We Three Kings* of Orient are
Trying to light a rubber cigar.'
It was loaded and exploded
Blowing them all afar.

We four Beatles of Liverpool are,
John in a taxi, Paul in a car,
George on a scooter, tooting his hooter,
Following Ringo Starr.

While Shepherds washed their socks by night
All seated round the tub,
A bar of Sunlight soap came down
And they began to scrub.

While shepherds watched their turnip tops
All boiling in the pot,
A lump of soot came rolling down
And spoilt the bloomin' lot.

Good King Wenceslas looked out
  On the Feast of Stephen;
A snowball hit him on the snout
  And made it all uneven.
Brightly shone his conk that night
  Though the pain was cruel,
Till the doctor came in sight
  Riding on a mu-oo-el.

Good King Wenceslas walked out
  In his mother's garden.
He bumped into a Brussels sprout
  And said 'I beg your pardon'.

Good King Wenceslas looked out
  When he was on 'telly',
Chased his page all round the screen
  And punched him in the belly.

Hark! the jelly babies sing,
Beecham's pills are just the thing,
They are gentle, meek and mild,
Two for a man and one for a child.
If you want to go to heaven
You must take a dose of seven;
If you want to go to hell,
Take the blinking box as well.

Nicky-nacky-noo

With my hands on my head, what have I here?
This is my brain-box, and nothing to fear.
Brain-box and nicky-nacky-noo,
That's what they taught me when I went to school.

With my hands on my eyes, what have I here?
These are my eye-blinkers, nothing to fear.
Eye-blinkers, brain-box, and nicky-nacky-noo,
That's what they taught me when I went to school.

With my hands on my nose, what have I here?
This is my nose-wiper, nothing to fear.
Nose-wiper, eye-blinkers,
Brain-box and nicky-nacky-noo,
That's what they taught me when I went to school.

With my hands on my mouth, what have I here?
This is my mouth-clicker, nothing to fear.
Mouth-clicker, nose-wiper, eye-blinkers,
Brain-box and nicky-nacky-noo,
That's what they taught me when I went to school.

With my hands on my chin, what have I here?
This is my chin-chopper, nothing to fear.
Chin-chopper, mouth-clicker,
Nose-wiper, eye-blinkers,
Brain-box and nicky-nacky-noo,
That's what they taught me when I went to school.

With my hands on my chest, what have I here?
This is my chest-protector, nothing to fear.
Chest-protector, chin-chopper,
Mouth-clicker, nose-wiper, eye-blinkers,
Brain-box and nicky-nacky-noo,
That's what they taught me when I went to school.

With my hands on my tum, what have I here?
This is my bread-box, and nothing to fear.
Bread-box, chest-protector,
Chin-chopper, mouth-clicker,
Nose-wiper, eye-blinkers,
Brain-box and nicky-nacky-noo,
That's what they taught me when I went to school.

With my hands on my knees, what have I here?
These are my knee-benders, nothing to fear.
Knee-benders, bread-box,
Chest-protector, chin-chopper,
Mouth-clicker, nose-wiper, eye-blinkers,
Brain-box and nicky-nacky-noo,
That's what they taught me when I went to school.

Traditional

Songs

(remembered by poet Seamus Heaney, as chanted on the way to and from school, in County Derry, Ireland, in the '40s).

One fine October's morning September last July
The moon lay thick upon the ground, the mud
                                        shone in the sky.
I stepped into a tramcar to take me across the sea,
I asked the conductor to punch my ticket, he
                                        punched my eye for me.

I fell in love with an Irish girl, she sang me an Irish
                                        dance,
She lived in Tipperary, just a few miles out of
                                        France.
The house it was a round one, the front was at the
                                        back,
It stood alone between two more, and it was
                                        whitewashed black.

Speech Day

Ladles and Jellyspoons,
I stand upon this speech to make a platform,
The train I arrived in has not yet come,
So I took a bus and walked.
I come before you
To stand behind you
And tell you something
I know nothing about.

Wycombe Abbey Song

When the holidays are over, and the term is well
                                                                    begun,
When our lesson books are put away, and the
                                                        morning's work is done,
Then we rush forth from the boot room, before the
                                                            clock strikes two,
For all of us are very keen to play lacrosse anew.

> *Chorus*
> Pass, catch, pass again. Keep it in the air.
> Now the centre's caught it, so down the field
>   we tear.

Now the hockey season follows and our sticks are
                                                            routed out,
When we've bullied at the centre, we begin to slash
                                                                    about.
We're fighting for our honour, for we want to win
                                                                the cup,
And the lusty shouts around us bid us not to give it
                                                                        up.

74

Chorus
HIC, HAC, HOC away, set it on the roll.
Pass it down to somebody and quickly shoot a
goal.

But the summer term is best for we are out from
morn to night,
Then we run out to play cricket as soon as it is light.
And we lie beneath the beeches when the sun is
overhead,
Then cricket in the evening till it's time to go to bed.

Chorus
Slog, run, run again, you're running up the
score.
Now do look out for catches. How's that for
leg before?

Written in 1902

School Song of Godolphin and Latimer School, Hammersmith

Rising early in the morning we proceed to Iffley
Road
Every girl herself adorning with a scarlet duffle
hood.

   Each is fearful lest too late
   She should come inside the gate.
   By the Staff-room we foregather
   Or perchance to read the weather
(Take a friend along for luck in either case).
When the dinner-money's checked
   All the home-work we collect,
Alphabetically, every book in place.
So very soon our lessons have begun,
We hope we shan't forget them everyone.
First of all we try to wrestle with some French,
And then we have to give our minds a wrench
To penetrate the mystery of Elizabethan history;
It's a rather tiresome business, we forget the names
and dates.

   Then the break bell makes us hurry,
   All is bustle, haste and scurry
To the table where we drink our milk provided by
the State.

   Thus refreshed we go to battle
   With hard problems about cattle.
'If six cows could eat a bale of hay, how much could
sixty eat?'

   Spend a little time in singing
   Or perhaps some minutes clinging
To the ropes in the gymnasium, with the aid of
hands and feet.

There's a long, long queue for dinner
(Every moment we feel thinner)
But we have a little gossip on the way.
Then we eat our lunch and chatter,
(Every moment growing fatter)
Though there's never time for all we have to say.
But the bell rings loud and long at just 2.10.
And hard at work each girl may soon be then.
Some learn how they should choose a piece of meat
And how to cook and make it fit to eat.

Others brush and pencil bearing
To the Art Room swift repairing
Draw and paint familiar figures (they can do it
                                rather well).

Some spend afternoons at science
Learn to use each weird appliance
And on the air comes floating many a strange and
                                wondrous smell.

After school it is a pleasure
To play hockey in full measure
Watch a match or practise singing, tune our fiddles,
                                join debate.

Then in shine, or shower or rain,
For the trolley bus or train
With our harrowing thoughts of homework we
                                go hurrying through the gate.

Chorus So we hail the 4th of May
        When we keep the school's birthday
        With dance and song and music and
                                with celebrations meet.
        It's a privilege and pleasure
        Which we treasure beyond measure
For the Dolphin school's delightful and it's very
                                hard to beat.

Pontefract and District High School School Song

It isn't only lessons
We come to school to learn,
E'en here we know the changes
Of Fortune, kind or stern.
We cannot all gain prizes
We can't win every game,
But though we're disappointed,
We love School just the same.

But one day we must leave it
And 'mid the world's stern strife
We'll know another teacher,
The great Headmistress Life.
Then may our old School's honour
Be still our proudest boast,
And may we e'er prove worthy
Of Her who taught us most.

SCHOOL DINNERS

TODAYS
MENU
COOKS
FLUFFY
DUMPLINGS

A Child's Grace

Here a little child I stand
Heaving up my either hand;
Cold as paddocks though they be,
Here I lift them up to Thee,
For a benison to fall
On our meat and on us all. Amen.
Robert Herrick

Dinner Lady

'Hold your plate a little nearer, dear,
if you want any gravy. – Someone's 'ere
changing the electric, all the plugs,
I couldn't boil the water up – those mugs
are there to put yer tea in, Jean. –
Hey! Mighty Mouse, where've you been
to get in such an awful dirty mess?
Go back and wash your face again! Who'd guess
you'd got a mother and a house an' home?
I've never ever seen you use a comb.
– As I was saying, couldn't even heat it. –
What d'you think we're here for? You must eat it!
– I says to 'im, not Mr H, – ter Bob,
"You gotta fix it now, it's your job
to keep things working 'ere; and we'll do ours
if you do yours, O.K.?" What dinner hours
do we get, me or you? When I'm through
I can't put me feet up, no more can you,

as like as not the rotten bus is late . . . –
Watch it, lad! Hold still, let's 'ave your plate.
– or all the shops 'ave shut before we're free
and then it's time to cook again for tea
and feed our own at 'ome, to fill his belly,
wash it up again while they watch telly
and still a pile of ironing to be done . . . –
Give it 'ere, that's cabbage, my ol' son.
No! Shepherd's pie, my pet, not sheep!
You funny child! – They make you weep.
God knows the kind of things they eat at 'ome,
no wonder some are only skin and bone,
with biscuits, crisps and pop an' sweets an' all
I don't think some mums cook their food at all. –
Don't push like that up there, stand still!
We'll not be serving seconds, not until
you let those other girls come through, and then
just to those as can behave . . . and when
you can stop that yelling at the back.
– Roll on Sunday, I say! – Shirley Black,
get that hair of yours from off the cheese!
Warren, use your hanky when you sneeze!
– Do their parents teach them anything?
You often wonder. – Sharon, will you bring
those dirty plates up when you queue for sweet?
– D'you know, half the kids that live in our street
don't get in till after ten at night?
Small wonder they look a pathetic sight
in morning school. But still, one thing that's good,
they get their midday dinners free. Hot food
is just what this lot need. – Let's 'ave that spoon.
– They do look better in the afternoon!'

Jane Whittle

Dinner Lady

I kissed the dinner lady
In a strange romantic dream.
Her cheeks blushed prettily
As strawberries with cream.

I kissed the dinner lady
And in my sleep I sighed.
I stroked her hair, as sooty black
As mushroom's underside.

I kissed the dinner lady,
My eyes closed quietly.
Like cool and fresh green watercress
Her clear eyes looked at me.

I kissed the dinner lady
As I lay drowsily,
She smiled at me with teeth as white
As crisp blanched celery.

I kissed the dinner lady
In a sleepy reverie.
Her lips were cool as lettuce leaves
As she pressed them on to me.

Now I kiss the dinner lady
Every meal–time of my life.
She is my cordon bleu girl
She is my loving wife.

Robert Sparrow

School Dinners

You go to school dinners,
You sit side by side,
You cannot escape –
Many have tried.
You look at the gravy,
All lumpy and still,
If that doesn't get you
The custard will.

Sent in by Philip Moody (aged 9)

School dinners, school dinners,
Burnt baked beans, burnt baked beans,
Sloppy semolina, sloppy semolina,
I feel sick,
Get a bucket quick.

Beans, beans, good for the heart,
The more you eat, the more you fart,
The more you fart, the better you feel,
So let's have beans for every meal.

The sausage is a cunning bird
With feathers long and wavy;
It swims about the frying pan
And makes its nest in gravy.

Apple crumble makes you rumble,
Apple tart makes you fart,
Apple snow makes you go,
Apple bun makes you run,
Apple pie makes you sigh,
Apple cake makes you ache.

There was a young lad of St Just
Who ate apple pie till he bust;
    It wasn't the fru-it
    That caused him to do it,
What finished him off was the crust.

Cherry Stones

*This is the rhyme you recite when counting
the cherry stones left on your plate.*

Who will I marry?
Tinker Tailor Soldier Sailor Rich Man
Poor Man Beggarman Thief
What will his name be?
A B C D . . .
What will I drive to Church in?
Coach Carriage Wheelbarrow Donkeycart.
What will I wear?
Silk Satin Cotton Rags.
Boots Shoes Sandals Clogs.
What will I live in?
Big House Little House Pigsty Barn.
How many children will I have?
1 2 3 4 . . .

Blotting Paper Pudding

Blotting paper pudding's a dish fit for a queen,
The mixture of ingredients, it really must be seen;
There's best black ink and gunpowder, and sealing
                                    wax as well,
And smudgy chalk, pink white and blue – the
                                    method now I'll tell.

For blotting paper pudding's a dish fit for a queen,
The way you set about it, it really must be seen.
You tear it up, and mix it up, and slosh it all about,
You give a stir, and take a sup, and then let out a
                                    shout –

Oh! blotting paper pudding's a dish fit for a queen,
A stranger dish you'll never find, it really must be
                                    seen
The cooking is the tricky bit, it's really quite an art,
The time and heat must be just right, before you
                                    make a start,

Then blotting paper pudding's a dish fit for a queen,
The recipe is quite unique, it really must be seen.
The taste is so astonishing, I'm sure you will agree,
It's sour, and sharp, and powdery, and bitter as can
be.

But blotting paper pudding's a dish fit for a queen,
My best invention ever, it really must be seen,
And when the work has all been done, and you can
feast your eyes,
I know you'll say, 'Well done, White Knight –
you've won the pudding prize!'

Jenny Craig

Humpty Dumpty sat on the wall
Eating black bananas.
Where d'you think he put the skins?
Down the king's pyjamas.

Sent in by Lucy Floyer (aged 4)

Poor Simon Benn

Poor Simon Benn
Poor Simon Benn
His sandwiches are frozen again,

All night long left in deep-freeze.
Now surely Mum intended to please
And not to vex, torment or tease.

It's no fun lunching
Cheek muscles bunching
Ice crystals crunching.

Mrs Benn please
Not steel-hard cheese
At zero degrees.

Please, Mrs Benn
Please, Mrs Benn
His sandwiches are frozen again.

Robert Sparrow

Mary ate jam,
Mary ate jelly,
Mary went home
With a pain in her –
Now don't get excited
Don't be misled
Mary went home
With a pain in her head.

Table Rules for Little Folk

In silence I must take my seat,
And give God thanks before I eat;
Must for my food in patience wait,
Till I am asked to hand my plate;
I must not scold, nor whine, nor pout,
Nor move my chair nor plate about;
With knife, or fork, or napkin ring,
I must not play, nor must I sing.
I must not speak a useless word,
For children should be seen, not heard;
I must not talk about my food,
Nor fret if I don't think it good;
I must not say, 'The bread is old,'
'The tea is hot,' 'The coffee's cold';
My mouth with food I must not crowd,
Nor while I'm eating speak aloud;
Must turn my head to cough or sneeze,
And when I ask, say 'If you please';
The tablecloth I must not spoil,
Nor with my food my fingers soil;
Must keep my seat whan I have done,
Nor round the table sport or run;
When told to rise, then I must put
My chair away with noiseless foot;
And lift my heart to God above,
In praise for all his wondrous love.

Anon (c. 1858)

Table Manners

The Goops they lick their fingers,
    And the Goops they lick their knives;
They spill their broth on the table-cloth;
    Oh, they live untidy lives.
The Goops they talk while eating,
    And loud and fast they chew,
So that is why I am glad that I
    Am not a Goop. Are you?

Gelett Burgess

Scottish Grace

Some hae meat that canna eat
    And some could eat that want it;
But we hae meat and we can eat,
    For which the Lord be thankit!

Anon

PLAYTIME

The Battle

Our janitor was tortured in the war,
The Boer War, I suppose,
So Pete reckoned we should have a battle
Down by the janny's hut.
It was fitting, I suppose.

I was Winston Churchill,
Bill was General Custer,
Joe was Julius Caesar
And Pete was Alfred the Great.
The one who burnt the cakes, I suppose.

Our janny was Adolf Hitler.
Our janny was Attila the Hun,
Our janny was Sitting Bull
And Wilfred, the school dog, was
His horse, I suppose.

In the dead of night
We circled our janitor's hut.
Joe had nicked some matches from his dad
And we flicked them through the dark,
Instead of bullets, I suppose.

Our janny's hut caught fire
And burned to the ground as we fled.
The night's silence returned,
Interrupted only by a far-off howling.
Wilfred, the school dog, I suppose.

Benjamin Bolt

Children's Song

Johnnie Crack and Flossie Snail
Kept their baby in a milking pail
Flossie Snail and Johnnie Crack
One would pull it out and one would put it back
O it's my turn now said Flossie Snail
To take the baby from the milking pail
And it's my turn now said Johnnie Crack
To smack it on the head and put it back

Johnnie Crack and Flossie Snail
Kept their baby in a milking pail
One would put it back and one would pull it out
And all it had to drink was ale and stout
For Johnnie Crack and Flossie Snail
Always used to say that stout and ale
Was *good* for a baby in a milking pail

Dylan Thomas (from 'Under Milk Wood')

Dips – to Start a Game

Dip!
Ickery, ahry, oary, ah,
Biddy, barber, oary, sah,
Peer, peer, mizter, meer,
Pit, pat, out one.

Eeny, meeny, miney, mo,
Sit the baby on the po,
When he's done,
Wipe his bum,
Tell his mummy what he's done.

Oh deary me,
Mother caught a flea,
Put it in the kettle
To make a cup of tea.
The flea jumped out,
And bit mother's snout,
In came daddy
With his shirt hanging out.

Paddy on the railway
Picking up stones;
Along came an engine
And broke Paddy's bones.
Oh, said Paddy,
That's not fair.
Pooh, said the engine-driver,
I don't care.

Hickety pickety i sillickety
Pompalorum jig,
Every man who has no hair
Generally wears a wig.
One, two, three,
Out goes he.

Eenty, teenty, orry, ram, tam, toosh,
Ging in alow the bed, and catch a wee fat moose.
Cut it up in slices, and fry it in a pan,
Mind and keep the gravy for the wee fat man.

Ip, dip, dalabadi,
Dutch cheese, santami,
Santa mi, dalabadi,
Sham.

One-ery, oo-ry, ick-ry, an,
Bipsy, bopsy, little Sir Jan,
Queery, quaury,
Virgin Mary,
Nick, tick, toloman tick,
O-U-T, out,
Rotten, totten, dish-clout,
Out jumps – He.

Mickey Mouse bought a house,
What colour did he paint it?
Shut your eyes and think.
– RED.
R-E-D spells red,
And out you must go for saying so
With a clip across your ear-hole.

Hinty, minty, cuty, corn,
Apple seed, and apple thorn,
Wire, briar, limber lock,
Three geese in a flock.
One flew east, and one flew west,
One flew over the cuckoo's nest.
       Up on yonder hill.
That is where my father dwells;
He has jewels, he has rings,
He has many pretty things.
He has a hammer with two nails,
He has a cat with twenty tails.
Strike Jack, lick Tom!
       Blow the bellows, old man!

Clapping Games

Who stole the buns from the bakery shop?
Number one stole the buns from the bakery shop.
Who, me?
Yes, you!
Couldn't have been me,
Number two stole the buns from the bakery shop.
Who, me?
Yes, you!
Couldn't have been me,
Number three stole the buns from the bakery
shop. . .

Um pom pay carolay carolester
Um pom pay carolay
Ickidideely so far lee
Ickidideely pouf pouf.

I am Popeye the sailor man – full stop –
I live in a caravan – full stop –
And when I go swimming
I kiss all the women
I am Popeye the sailor man –
Full stop, full stop,
Comma, comma,
Dash, Dash.

I went to a Chinese restaurant to buy a loaf of bread,
He asked me what my surname was, and this is
                                    what I sai-ai-aid,

'Zom pom poodle
Allawalie whisky
Chinese chopsticks
Indian squawful
O-o-o-o-o
How!'

Under the bamboo,
Under the sea,
Boom, boom, boom!
True love for me, my darling,
True love for you.
And when we're married
We'll raise a family,
And so it's under the bamboo,
Under the sea.

Tommy broke a bottle
And blamed it on me.
I told Ma
Ma told Pa
Tommy got a whacking
On his Oom pa pa!

I am a girl guide dressed in blue,
These are the actions I can do –
Salute to the captain,
Curtsey to the queen,
Show my panties to the football team.

I had the German measles
I had them really bad,
They wrapped me up in blankets
And threw me in the van,
The van was very shaky
I nearly fell out,
But when I got to hospital
I heard the children shout –
'Mummy, Daddy, take me home
I've been here a year or so.'
In came Dr Alastair
Sliding down the banister,
Half way down he split his pants
Now he's doing the ballet dance.

Jumping Game

Cat's got the measles,
Dog's got the flu,
Chicken's got the chicken pox,
And so have you.

All sent in by girls from
Downton Primary School

Child's Bouncing Song

Molly Vickers
wets her knickers,
Georgie's father's big and black,
cream on Sunday
milk on Monday,
I'm the cock of all the back.

Tell me who's a
bigger boozer
Mister Baker beats them all,
from his lorry
watch him hurry,
touch the ground and touch the wall.

Who're the gentry
down our entry – Mrs Smith's got two TV's.
What if her coat
is a fur coat,
all her kids are full of fleas.

Joan loves Harry,
Jack will marry
Edna when they both grow up,
I'll announce it,
bounce bounce bounce it,
our dog Whisker's had a pup.

High and low and
to and fro and
down the street and up the hill,
Mrs Cuthbert's
husband snuffed it,
she got nothing from his will.

Mister, mister,
Shirley's sister
won a prize on Blackpool prom,
mam'll smother
our kid brother
when the school inspectors come.

Skip and hopping
I'm off shopping,
Tuesday night it's pie for tea,
please to take this
ball and make this
song a bouncing song for me.

Tony Connor

Ball Bouncing

Bounce ball! Bounce ball!
One, two, three.
Underneath my right leg
And round about my knee.
Bounce ball! Bounce ball!
Bird–or–bee
Flying from the rose-bud
Up into the tree.

Bounce ball! Bounce ball!
Fast-you-go.
Underneath my left leg
And round about my toe.
Bounce ball! Bounce ball!
Butt-er-fly
Flying from the rose-bud
Up into the sky.

Long-legged Italy
Kicked poor Sicily
Into the middle of the Mediterranean Sea.
Austria was Hungary,
Took a bit of Turkey,
Dipped it in Greece,
Fried it in Japan,
And ate it off China.

Skipping Rhymes

A frog walked into a public house,
   and asked for a pint of beer.
'Where's your money?'
  'In my pocket.'
'Where's your pocket?'
  'I forgot it.'
'Well, please walk out.'

        Eaver Weaver, chimney sweeper,
          Had a wife and couldn't keep her,
        Had another, didn't love her,
          Up the chimney he did shove her.

Tiddly Wink the barber,
Went to shave his father,
   The razor slip
   and cut his lip,
Tiddly Wink the barber.

        Good King Wenceslas,
        Knocked a bobby senseless,
        Right in the middle of
        Marks and Spencers.

Julius Caesar,
The Roman Geezer,
Squashed his wife
With a lemon squeezer.

All sent in by Ceri Broomhead (aged 11)

One o'clock, two o'clock, three o'clock, four,
In comes (Polly) through the door.
Five o'clock, six o'clock, seven o'clock, eight,
Out goes (Polly) through the gate.

I like coffee, I like tea,
I like the boys and they like me.
So tell your ma to hold her tongue
'Cos she had a boy when she was young.
And tell your pa to do the same,
'Cos he was the one who changed her name.

Jelly on the plate, jelly on the plate
Wibble wobble wibble wobble
Jelly on the plate.
Custard on the spoon, custard on the spoon
Lick it off, lick it off
Custard on the spoon.
Sausage in the pan, sausage in the pan
One goes pop
And the other goes bang.

Redcurrant, blackcurrant, raspberry tart,
Tell me the name of your sweetheart:
A B C D . . .

One two, buckle my shoe
Three four, shut the door
Five six, pick up sticks
Seven eight, lay them straight
Nine ten, a big fat hen
Eleven twelve, dig and delve
Thirteen fourteen, maids a-courting
Fifteen sixteen, maids a-milking
Seventeen eighteen, maids a-baking
Nineteen twenty, my plate's empty:
Please give me some *tea!*

1 2 3 4 5 6 7,
All good children go to heaven.
Penny on the water
Tuppence on the sea
Threepence on the railway,
And *out goes she!*

One two three *O'Lary*
I spy sister *Mary*
Sitting on a *pompalary*
Eating chocolate *wafers*.

Salt Mustard Vinegar Pepper,
French Almond Rock.
Bread and butter for your supper
That's all mother's got.
Fish and chips and coca cola,
Pig's head and trout.
Bread and butter for your supper,
O.U.T. spells *out*.

Peter *Pan* bread and *jam*
Marmalade and *treacle*.
A bit for *you* and a bit for *me*
And *none* for naughty people.

I had a little *sausage*,
A little German *sausage*,
I put it in the pan for me *tea*.
I went out playing,
And I heard the sausage saying
Ellen, Ellen, Ellen, come in for your tea.

Charlie Chaplin washing up
Broke a basin and a cup.
How much did they cost?
10p – 20p – 30p – . . .

Teddy bear, teddy bear
Touch the ground.
Teddy bear, teddy bear
Turn around.
Teddy bear, teddy bear
Jump upstairs.
Teddy bear, teddy bear
Say your prayers.
Teddy bear, teddy bear
Blow out the light.
Teddy bear, teddy bear
Say goodnight!

Two, four, six, eight,
Mary at the cottage gate,
Eating cherries off a plate.
Two, four, six, eight.

All in together
This fine weather.
When it's your birthday,
Please run out.
    January, February, March . . .
All in together
This fine weather.
When it's your birthday
Please run in.
    1st, 2nd, 3rd . . .

Nebuchadnezzar the King of the Jews
Bought his wife a pair of shoes.
When the shoes began to wear
Nebuchadnezzar began to swear.

Over the garden wall
I let the baby fall.
My mother came out
And gave me a shout
Over the garden wall.

Over the garden wall
I let the baby fall.
My father came out
And gave me a clout
Over the garden wall.

Belfast Skipping Song

Datsie-dotsie, miss the rope, you're outie-o,
If you'd've been, where I'd have been,
You wouldn't have been put outie-o,
All the money's scarce, people out of workie-o,
Datsie-dotsie, miss the rope, you're outie-o.

Conkers

Conker Jeremy,
My first blow,
Conker Jack,
My first whack.

Ally, ally, onker,
My first conker,
Quack, quack,
My first smack.

Obbly, onker,
My first conker,
Obbly oh,
My first go.

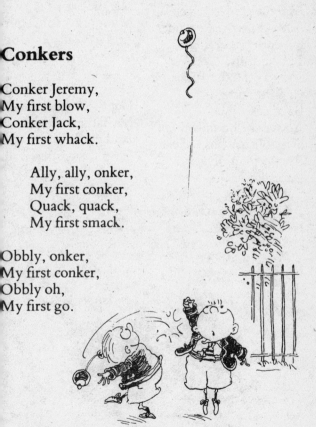

Winter

On Winter mornings in the playground
The boys stand huddled,
Their cold hands doubled
Into trouser pockets.
The air hangs frozen
About the buildings
And the cold is an ache in the blood
And a pain on the tender skin
Beneath finger nails.
The odd shouts
Sound off like struck iron
And the sun
Balances white
Above the boundary wall.
I fumble my bus ticket
Between numb fingers
Into a fag,
Take a drag
And blow white smoke
Into the December air.

Gareth Owen

Words

Sticks and stones
May break my bones
But words can never hurt me –
That is what I'm supposed to say.
But:
'One, two, three,
Bri–an Lee –
His mother picks his fleas,
She roasts them,
She toasts them,
They have them for their teas.'

Sticks and stones
May break my bones
But words can never hurt me –
That is what I say.

But:
'One, two, three,
Bri–an Lee
Went to sea,
A big fish swam up
Got him by the knee.
The boat turned over,
Brian couldn't swim.
I wonder whatever
Happened to him.'

Sticks and stones
May break my bones
But. . . .
'One, two, three,
Bri–an Lee
Went for a pee –
Never came back.
Found him later,
Put him in a sack.'

Sticks and stones. . . .
But. . . .
Words can prick,
Can pierce, can sting,
Can cut, can stab,
Can scar, can sling.
This is what I shout back:

'George Rudden
Is fat as a pig,
He eats so much pudden
His belly gets big.'

'Mary McVicker's
Brain's gone numb,
When she bends over
We can all see her bum.
She's forgot to put them on –
No–knickers
Mary McVickers.'

'Freddy Bell
's got feet that smell –
He won't change his socks.
Shut him in a cell,
Drop him down a well,
Nail him in a box.'

But. . . .
They won't clear off.
Nothing I say
Seems quite good enough
To hurt them as much
As they hurt me. . . .
Though I stand and shout
Till some mister comes out
And tells me to go away.

Sticks and stones
May break my bones –

With a pound of plaster
Your bones get better –
But once it's been heard,
Who forgets the Word?

Brian Lee

The Fight

The kick off is
I don't like him;
Nothing about him.
He's fat and soft;
Like a jellybaby he is.
Now he's never done nothing,
Not to me,
He wouldn't dare:
Nothing at all of anything like that.
I just can't stand him,
So I'll fight him
And I'll beat him,
I could beat him any day.

The kick off is, it's his knees:
They knock together,
They sock together.
And they're fat,
With veins that run into his socks
Too high.
Like a girl he is,
And his shorts,
Too long,
They look
All wrong,
Like a Mum's boy.
Then
He simpers and dimples,
Like a big lass he is;
So I'll fight him
Everyone beats him,
I could beat him any day.

For another thing it's his hair,
All smarmed and oily fair,
All silk and parted flat,
His Mum does it like that
With her flat hand and water,
All licked and spittled into place,
With the quiff all down his face.
And his satchel's new
With his name in blue
Chalked on it.
So I chalked on it,
'Trevor is a cissie'
On it.
So he's going to fight me,
But I'll beat him,
I could beat him any day.

There's a crowd behind the sheds
When we come they turn their heads
Shouting and laughing,
Wanting blood and a bashing.
Take off my coat, rush him,
Smash him, bash him
Lash him, crash him
In the head,
In the bread
Basket.

Crack, thwack,
He's hit me back
Shout and scream
'Gerroff me back,
Gerroff, gerroff!
You wait, I'll get you,
I could beat you any day!'

Swing punch, bit his hand.
Blood on teeth, blood on sand.
Buttons tear, shouts and sighs,
Running nose, tears in eyes.

I'll get him yet; smack him yet.
Smash his smile, teacher's pet.
Brow grazed by knuckle
Knees begin to buckle.
'Gerroff me arms you're hurtin' me!'
'Give in?'
'No.'
'Give in?'
'No. Gerroff me arms!'
'Give in?'
'No.'
'Give in?'
'GIVE IN?'
'NEVER.'
'GIVE IN?'
'OOOH GERROFF GERROFF.'
'GIVE IN?'
'I . . . give . . . in . . . yeah.'

Don't cry, don't cry,
Wipe tears from your eye.
Walk home all alone
In the gutters all alone.
Next time I'll send him flying,
I wasn't really trying;
I could beat him any day.

Gareth Owen

The Bully

One of the girls at Audrey's school
Would terrify the others.
She'd talk about a Creep that lurks
And of a Thing that smothers.

She'd tell them that she'd be in touch
(Unless they gave her stuff
Like necklaces and sharpeners)
With the beasts that acted tough.

The children were too scared to tell
And never explained fully
About this girl, whom we won't name,
Except to call her bully.

Fay Maschler

Hill Rolling

I kind of exploded inside,
and joy shot out of me.
I began my roll down the grassy hill.
I bent my knees up small, took a deep breath
and I was off.
My arms shot out sideways.
I gathered speed.
My eyes squinted.
Sky and grass, dazzle and dark.

I went on forever,
My arms were covered with dents,
holes, squashed grass.
Before I knew it I was at the bottom.
The game was over.
The door of the classroom closed behind me.
I can smell chalk dust, and hear the voice of teacher,
to make me forget my hill.

Andrew Taylor

SPORTS

FIRST YEAR
RUGBY
LESSON 1
THE TACKLE

I'm a Man

I'm a man.
   A grown up man?
A nearly man.
   A man in short trousers?
Short trouser man.
   Can you drive?
I walk to the park.
   A short trouser park keeper?
I'm a goalie.
   And can't touch the bar?
But I'm growing.
   Growing?
Bit by bit.
   A bit on the top?
To reach the bar.
   And a bit on the bottom?
To lengthen into longs.
   And then you'll be a bit of a park-keeper?
No. Then I'll be a goalie.
   In long trousers?
No. In shorts.
   I don't see the point.
Who asked you to?

Michael Rosen

Choosing Sides

First you stand in a bunch
Then it's decided
– though everybody already knows it –
that Rolf and Erik are going to choose
Rolf stands on one line
Erik stands on another
All of us others sit down by the fence
'Lars!' calls out Rolf
'Harold!' yells Erik!
'Emil!' 'Kent!' 'David!' 'Thomas!' 'Martin!'
Then it's only me left;
I go to Erik's team
that's already started dribbling the ball . . .

Siv Widerberg

Here are the Football Results

League Division Fun
Manchester United won, Manchester City lost.
Crystal Palace 2, Buckingham Palace 1
Millwall Leeds nowhere
Wolves 8 A cheese roll and had a cup of tea 2
Aldershot 3 Buffalo Bill shot 2
Evertonill, Liverpool's not very well either
Newcastle's Heaven Sunderland's a very nice place 2
Ipswhich one? You tell me.

Michael Rosen

Football Game

The blue sky
The gold and scarlet shirts
And black shorts
The football match began
Dashing movement
Thrilling, excitement,
Energy, lively,
Whistle, sweat,
Fierce attack
Hopeful,
Spectators cheering,
Bouncing ball
Dashing players
Whistle blows
Half time
Cool refreshments
No score yet
Half hour to go
Back on the field
To sweat and heat
Whistle blows

Off again
Zooming down the field
Goal at last
1–0 and ten minutes
to go
Spectators roaring
Brilliant play
Fierce attack
Whistle blows
Full time
We've won 1–0.

Roger Gibbs (aged 11)

The Pass

I was going like a rocket
When Pearson passed the ball.
I took it really cleanly
And astonished them all.

The last match of the season –
Vital that we score.
But should I pass to Armstrong,
Or go myself 'n make sure?

If I pass to Armstrong
He may drop it – he's a clot.
I'll go myself I reckon –
We need to win a lot.

But there's a massive forward
About to join the fray.
I think I'll pass to Armstrong –
We're bound to win that way.

But just as I made my mind up
And the ball to Armstrong tossed,
The referee blew his whistle,
The game finished, and we lost.

Benjamin Bolt

Cricketer

Light
as the flight
of a bird on the wing
my feet skim the grass
and my heart seems to sing:
'How green is the wicket.
It's cricket.
It's spring.'

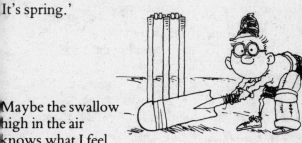

Maybe the swallow
high in the air
knows what I feel
when I bowl fast and follow
the ball's twist and bounce.
Maybe the cat
knows what I feel like, holding my bat
and ready to pounce.
Maybe the tree
so supple and yielding
to the wind's sway
then swinging back, gay,
might know the way
I feel when I'm fielding.

Oh, the bird, the cat and the tree:
they're cricket, they're me.

R. C. Scriven

There's a Breathless Hush in the Close Tonight

There's a breathless hush in the Close tonight –
Ten to make and the match to win –
A bumping pitch and a blinding light,
An hour to play and the last man in,
And it's not for the sake of a ribboned coat,
Or the selfish hope of a season's fame,
But his Captain's hand on his shoulder smote –
'Play up! play up! and play the game!'

The sand of the desert is sodden red, –
Red with the wreck of a square that broke; –
The gatling's jammed and the colonel dead,
And the regiment blind with the dust and smoke.
The river of death has brimmed its banks
And England's far and honour a name,
But the voice of a schoolboy rallies the ranks:
'Play up! play up! and play the game!'

Sir Henry Newbolt

I Ran for a Catch

I ran for a catch
    With the sun in my eyes, sir,
Being sure of a 'snatch'
    I ran for a catch . . .
Now I wear a black patch
    And a nose *such* a size, sir,
I ran for a catch
    With the sun in my eyes, sir.

Coulson Kernahan

The Name of the Game

'Catch the *ball*!' the teacher cried.
I ran, I jumped, I stretched, I tried.
I really did.
        – I missed.

'Useless!' she yelled. 'Silly girl!' she spat.
'What on earth d'you think you're playing at?'
'A game,' I said.
        – And wept.

Jenny Craig

Rounders

There once was a boy called Paul
Who couldn't throw a rounders ball.
When trying to throw,
His shoulder said 'No'.
What an awkward shoulder had Paul!

Howard Wilkinson (aged 9)

Games Lesson – Rounders

	Bowl from the bowler.
Batsman:	Whack!
Other fielders:	'Catch!'
	Missed.
	'Stupid, let me go there.'
Teacher:	'One rounder.'
	I feel so hopeless now.

Gail Harding (aged 9)

OUT OF SCHOOL

Voices

Oh, Cuckoo, Cuckoo away on Knockree,
'Tis well for yourself now you're idle and free,
For there you are gaming away on the hill,
And I'm in the schoolhouse obliged to sit still.
    Is it 'When will you come?'
    When I finish my sum.
    If the clock would strike four
    Then they'll open the door.

Let you call me then, Cuckoo, call out loud and I'll
                                come.
Away in the meadows the corncrakes shout
'Will you come now an' seek me? Come out, come
                                out.
I'm under the window, I'm close to the wall,
I'm holding the wall up for fear it would fall.
    Am I under your feet
    Or away in the wheat?
    Let you seek for me soon;
    I've been calling since noon.'
And it's here I sit working, nigh kilt with the heat.

The king has a right to make it a rule
That only old men should be sitting in school.
I'm moidhered with voices singing and humming,
'The hours are passing and when are you coming?'
    Just a minyit or more
    An' they'll open the door.
    When I've finished my sum
    Be aware! for I'll come.
Och! Now glory to goodness! the clock's striking
                                  four!

W. M. Letts

School's Out

Girls scream,
   Boys shout;
Dogs bark,
   School's out.

Cats run,
   Horses shy;
Into trees
   Birds fly.

Babes wake
   Open-eyed.
If they can,
   Tramps hide.

Old man,
   Hobble home;
Merry mites,
   Welcome.

W. H. Davies

Out of School

Four o'clock strikes
There's a rising hum,
Then the doors fly open
The children come.

With a wild cat-call
And a hop-scotch hop
And a bouncing ball
And a whirling top.

Grazing of knees
A hair-pull and a slap,
A hitched up satchel,
A pulled down cap,

Bully boys reeling off
Hurt ones squealing off,
Aviators wheeling off,
Mousy ones stealing off,

Woollen gloves for chilblains,
Cotton rags for snufflers,
Pig-tails, coat-tails,
Tails of mufflers.

Machine gun cries
A kennelful of snarlings
A hurricane of leaves
A treeful of starlings,

Thinning away now
By some and some,
Thinning away, away,
All gone home.

Hal Summers

Walking from School

Walking from school is a consummate art:
Which routes to follow to avoid the gangs,
Which paths to find that lead, circuitous,
To leafy squirrel haunts and plopping ponds,
For dreams of Archibald and Tiger Tim;
Which hiding-place is safe, and when it is;
What time to leave to dodge the enemy.
I only once was trapped. I knew the trap –
I heard it in their tones: 'Walk back with us.'
I knew they weren't my friends; but that soft voice
Wheedled me from my route to cold Swain's Lane.
There in a holly bush they threw me down,
Pulled off my shorts, and laughed and ran away;
And, as I struggled up, I saw grey brick,
The cemetery railings, and the tombs.

John Betjeman
(from 'Summoned by Bells')

11 Bus

As usual the old bulky brigade bumbling,
Entered the bus stumbling,
Hands in pockets, moaning and mumbling,
For fare fumbling,
But boys behind them bundling,
With long, straight-laced boots trundling,
Set the fumbling, mumbling, bumbling, tumbling
                              old maids grumbling.
With a sudden hefty whack
The bundling, trundling boys were crumbling,
Before an umbrella.

S. Hale

Top-secret School

Five days a week, except when irksome ears
Or churchyard coughs confine the little dears,

Sealed when it's wet or swaddled when it's cool,
The tots are taken to their Infant School.

Some trudge on leaden feet or lag behind,
Feasting their eyes on slugs and things they find.

Some shoot ahead or steer a curving course,
Claiming to be a capsule or a horse,

But most arrive by car and, having come,
Commingle with a penetrating hum.

Till noon they stay and then they get dismissed
And carted home and, for the most part, kissed,

And, at some point in these affecting scenes,
Changed from their blazers into jodhs or jeans.

What happens in between, what painting pads
They splodge with green-haired mums and noseless
dads,

What mimes and rhymes and roundelays they try
Or if they simply sit and multiply,

Or play pontoon or plant unceasing cress
Or fly to Mars is anybody's guess.

Brash elders bravely seeking to obtain
Enlightenment on matters in this vein

Find their demands invariably met
With a shrill-giggled 'Golly! I forget.'

Daniel Pettiward

After School

Hey little ghostie,
I spy you peeping there.
You thought I didn't see you
Taking the school room air.

Nice little ghostie
In your school pinafore
Neatly darned and ironed
That you always wore.

Pale little ghostie
Standing open-eyed
In the dark half shadow
By the cupboard's side.

Well, little ghostie
Puzzled at what you see?
Blocks, bricks, discs and cubes,
A plastic miscellany.

So little ghostie
Did you chant A – B – C?
Scratch on a squeaky slate
To learn calligraphy?

Poor little ghostie
Did you hold your fingers bent?
Stitching at a sampler?
And catechise for Lent?

Tell, little ghostie
Are children still the same
Jumping to a skipping rhyme?
Was that your favourite game?

Now little ghostie
What did you seek to know
In this tired old school room
From a hundred years ago?

Quiet little ghostie
Creeping without a sound,
Peering, prying slyly –
I don't mind if you're around.

Robert Sparrow

Parents' Evening

Tonight your mum and dad go off to school.
The classroom's empty.
Rabbit and gerbil sleep.
Your painting's with the others on the wall,
And all the projects you have ever done,
The long-since-finished and the just-begun,
Are ranged on desks.
Your books are in a pile.
'He gets his fractions right,' your teacher says.
Your mother reads your 'news',
Is pleased to find you've prominently listed
The sticky pudding that you liked last Tuesday.

Suppose one evening you could go along
To see how mum and dad had spent their days,
What sort of work would you find up on show?
Bus-loads of people,
Towers of coins,
Letters to fill a hundred postmen's sacks,
Hayricks of dust from offices and houses,
Plates, cakes, trains, clothes,
Stretches of motorways and bridges,
Aeroplanes and bits of ships,
Bulldozers and paperclips,
'Cellos and pneumatic drills.
A noise to make the sleepy gerbil stir.

Shirley Toulson

Homework

Homework sits on top of Sunday, squashing
Sunday flat.
Homework has the smell of Monday, homework's
very fat
Heavy books and piles of paper, answers I don't
know.
Sunday evening's almost finished, now I'm going
to go
Do my homework in the kitchen. Maybe just a
snack,
Then I'll sit right down and start as soon as I run
back
For some chocolate sandwich cookies. Then I'll
really do
All that homework in a minute. First I'll see what
new
Show they've got on television in the living room.
Everybody's laughing there, but misery and gloom
And a full refrigerator are where I am at.
I'll just have another sandwich. Homework's very
fat.

Russell Hoban

A Little Mistake

I studied my tables over and over, and backwards
                              and forwards, too;
But I couldn't remember six times nine, and I didn't
                              know what to do,
Till sister told me to play with my doll, and not to
                              bother my head.
'If you call her 'fifty-four' for a while, you'll learn it
                              by heart,' she said.

So I took my favourite Mary Ann (though I thought
                              'twas a dreadful shame
To give such a perfectly lovely child such a perfectly
                              horrid name),
And I called her 'My dear little fifty-four' a hundred
                              times, till I knew
The answer of six times nine as well as the answer of
                              two times two.

Next day, Elizabeth Wrigglesworth, who always
                              acts so proud,
Said 'Six times nine is fifty-two,' and I nearly
                              laughed aloud!
But I wished I hadn't when teacher said, 'Now,
                              Dorothy, tell if you can.'
For I thought of my doll, and – oh dear, oh dear! – I
                              answered 'Mary Ann'!

A. M. Platt

No more days of school,
No more days of sorrow,
No more days of YAK YAK YAK
'Cos we're off tomorrow.

No more pencils, no more books,
No more teacher's ugly looks,
No more things that bring us sorrow
'Cos we won't be here tomorrow.

We break up, we break down,
We don't care if the school falls down.
This time next week where shall we be?
Out of the gates of misery!
No more Latin, no more French,
No more sitting on the hard old bench.
No more cabbages filled with slugs,
No more drinking out of dirty old mugs.
No more spiders in my tea,
Making googly eyes at me.
Kick up tables, kick up chairs,
Kick old teacher down the stairs,
If that does not serve her right,
Blow her up with dynamite.

Saturdays

Real
Genuine
Saturdays
Like marbles
Conkers
Sweet new potatoes
Have their especial season
Are all morning
With midday at five o'clock.
True Saturdays
Are borrowed from early Winter
And the left overs
Of Autumn sunshine days
But separate from days of snow.
The skies dine on dwindles of smoke
Where leafy plots smoulder
With small fires.
Sunday meat is bought
And late
Large, white loaves
From little corner shops.
People passing
Wave over garden walls,
Greengrocers and milkmen are smiled upon
And duly paid.
It is time for the chequered tablecloth
And bowls of soup.
And early on
We set out with some purpose
Through only

Lovely Saturday,
Under skies
Like sun-shot water,
For the leccy train
And the Match in Liverpool.

Gareth Owen

Saturdays

When I was ten, a Saturday
Stretched its barefoot, hungry way
From waking up and hearing Mum
And seeing if the post had come
To breakfast . . . curly bacon . . . then . . .
Begin again
With fried bread central on the plate . . .
Still only half past eight.

Then the long, sweet freedom of the day
For play
And pocket money.
Every Saturday was sunny.

Gwen Dunn

Hymn for Saturday

Now's the time for mirth and play,
Saturday's an holiday;
Praise to heaven unceasing yield,
I've found a lark's nest in the field.

A lark's nest, then your playmate begs
You'd spare herself and speckled eggs;
Soon she shall ascend and sing
Your praises to the eternal King.

Christopher Smart

Sitting on Trev's back wall on the last day of the holidays trying to think of something to do

We sit and squint on Trev's back wall
By the clothes line
Watching the shirts flap
Hearing the shirts slap
In the sunshine.
There's nothing much to do at all
But try to keep cool
And it's our last day
Of the holiday
Tomorrow we're back at school.

We keep suggesting games to play
Like Monopoly.
But you need a day

If you want to play
It properly.
We played for four hours yesterday
Between rainfalls
In Trev's front room
That's like a tomb
And always smells of mothballs.

Says Trev, 'Why don't we kick a ball
Over the Wasteground?'
But the weather's got
Far too hot
To run around.
John kicks his heels against the wall
Stokesy scratches his head
I head a ball
Chalk my name on the wall
While Trev pretends that he's dead.

Says John, 'Let's go to the cinder track
And play speedway.
We can go by the dykes
It's not far on our bikes
I'll lead the way.'
'My saddlebag's all straw at the back
Being used by blackbirds.'
'And there's something unreal
About my fixed wheel
It only drives me backwards.'

Trev's Granny chucks out crusts of bread
For the sparrows
While their black cat

Crouches flat
Winking in the shadows.
Trev leaps up and bangs his head
With a sudden roar.
'We could er . . . . .,' he says.
'We could er . . . . .,' he says.
And then sits down once more.

'Let's play Releevo on the sands,'
Says John at last.
We set out with a shout
But his mother calls out,
'It's gone half-past
Your tea's all laid, you wash your hands
They're absolutely grey.'
'Oh go on Mum
Do I have to come
We were just going out to play.'

Old Stokes trails home and pulls a face.
'I'll see you Trev.'
'See you John.'
'See you Trev.'
'See you tonight the usual place.'
'Yes right, all right.'
'Don't forget.'
'You bet.'
'See you then tonight.'
'See you.'
'See you.'
'See
You.'

Gareth Owen

The Porter

I'd like to be a porter, and always on the run.
Calling out, 'Stand aside!' and asking leave of none.
Shoving trucks on people's toes, and having
                                        splendid fun;
Slamming all the carriage doors and locking every
                                                    one –
And, when they asked to be let in, I'd say, 'It can't
                                            be done.'
    But I wouldn't be a porter if . . .
            The luggage weighed a ton.
                Would you?

                                        C. J. Dennis

The Barber

I'd like to be a barber, and learn to shave and clip,
Calling out, 'Next, please!' and pocketing my tip.
All day you'd hear my scissors going, 'Snip, Snip,
                                                Snip!'
I'd lather people's faces, and their noses I would grip
While I shaved most carefully along the upper lip.
    But I wouldn't be a barber if . . .
            The razor was to slip.
                Would you?

                                        C. J. Dennis

What Would You Like to be When You Grow Up, Little Girl?

I'd like to be a model girl, lithe and long and lean;
I'd like to be a TV star, shining from the screen:

I'd like to be an actress, and strut upon the stage;
I'd like to be a poet, printed on this page:

I'd like to be a busy nurse, smoothing down the
                                             sheets;
I'd like to be an usherette, and show you to your
                                              seats:

I'd like to be a banker, and make a lot of money;
I'd like to be a bee-keeper, and bask on bread and
                                             honey:

I'd like to be a dancer, and dance the disco beat;
I'd like to be a traffic warden, storming down the
                                             street:

I'd like to be a hairdresser, with blower, brush and
                                              comb;
I'd like to be a Romany, the whole wide world to
                                              roam:

I'd like to be an air hostess, and soar across the seas;
I'd like to be a doctor, and dose you when you
                                            sneeze:

I'd like to be in parliament, and speak a speech for
you
I'd like to be a High Court Judge, and try a case or
two:

I'd like to be a teacher, and quell you with one look;
I'd like to be an artist, and illustrate this book:

I'd like to be a gymnast, and balance on a bar;
I'd like to be a grand chauffeur, and drive a dashing
car:

I'd like to be a skater, racing round a rink;
I'd like to be just *anything* . . . I think!

Jenny Craig

Career

I'd rather drive an engine than
Be a little gentleman
I'd rather go shunting and hooting
Then hunting and shooting.

Daniel Pettiward

Psychological Prediction

I think little Louie will turn out a crook. He
Puts on rubber gloves when stealing a cookie.

Virginia Brasier

Jobs

Pete wants to be a computer operator
He read about it in a book
But you need to know about
Silicon chips
And scientific gobbledy-gook.

Joe wants to be a footballer
A goalie, a really big star
But you need to like fast cars
And fast women
Whatever they are.

Mike wants to be astronaut
He saw them on the box
But you need to wear them
Goldfish bowls and plastic
Shoes and socks.

But when I'm asked myself, by you
I whistle and look blank
Could I really drive a train
Put out fires or
Sit in a bank?

I don't really want to do anything
I just can't find a niche
Oh, one thing I hadn't thought of
I know what I'll do
I'll teach.

Benjamin Bolt

Index of titles

Index of first lines

Acknowledgements

The author and publishers would like to thank the following people for giving permission to include in this anthology material which is their copyright. The publishers have made every effort to trace copyright holders. If we have inadvertently omitted to acknowledge anyone we should be most grateful if this could be brought to our attention for correction at the first opportunity.

Karen Aldous and Lewknor School for 'The New Boy'.
Angus and Robertson (UK) Limited for 'The Porter' and 'The Barber' by C. J. Dennis from *A Book for Kids*.
Bogle L'Ouverture Publications Limited for 'Confusion' by Odette Thomas from *Rain Falling, Sun Shining*.
Jonathan Cape Limited on behalf of Roger McGough for 'First Day at School', 'The Lesson', 'A Good Poem', 'Streemin' and 'Nooligan' from *In the Classroom*; on behalf of the Executors of the W. H. Davies Estate for 'School's Out' from *Complete Poems*; and on behalf of Fay Maschler for 'The Bully' from *A Child's Book of Manners*.
Tony Connor for 'Child's Bouncing Song' from *Lodgers*, published by Oxford University Press.
Graeme Curry for 'The Pass', 'The Battle' and 'Jobs' by Benjamin Bolt.
The Literary Trustees of Walter de la Mare and The Society of Authors as their representative for 'The Dunce' by Walter de la Mare from *Peacock Pie*.
André Deutsch for 'I'm a Man' by Michael Rosen from *Mind Your Own Business* and 'Maths Problems' by Alvin Schwartz from *A Twister of Twists*.
Dennis Dobson Publishers for 'The ABC' by Spike Milligan from *The Little Pot Boiler*.
Mrs Gwen Dunn for 'I Went Back' and 'Saturdays' from *The Live-long Day*, published by BBC Radio for Schools.
The Feminist Press for 'Choosing Sides' by Siv Widerberg from *I'm Like Me*, translated by Verne Moberg, copyright © 1968, 1969, 1970, 1971 Siv Widerberg; translation copyright © 1973 Verne Moberg.
Roger Gibbs for 'Football Game' from *The Live-long Day*, published by BBC Radio for Schools.
Elizabeth M. Graham-Yooll for 'Morning Prayers'.
Hamish Hamilton Limited for 'Exercise Book' by Jacques Prévert, translated by Paul Dehn, from *The Fern on the Rock*, copyright © Dehn Enterprises Limited 1965, 1976.
David Higham Associates for 'Timothy Winters' by Charles Causley from *Collected Poems*, published by Macmillan; for 'School Bell' by Eleanor Farjeon from *The Children's Bells*, published by Oxford University Press; for 'Homework' by Russell Hoban from *Egg Thoughts*; and for 'Children's Song' by Dylan Thomas from *Under Milk Wood*, published by Dent.
Hodder & Stoughton Children's Books for 'Going to School in the Country' and 'Going to School in the Town' by Leonard Clark from *The Singing Time*.

Lutterworth Press for 'The English Language' by Harry Hemsley from *Imagination*.

Brian Lee and Penguin Books Limited for 'Words' from *Late Home*.

John Murray (Publishers) Limited for 'Walking from School' from *Summoned by Bells* by John Betjeman.

Gareth Owen and Penguin Books Limited for 'Our School', 'Winter', 'The Fight', 'Saturdays' and 'Sitting on Trev's back wall on the last day of the holidays trying to think of something to do' from *Salford Road*.

Oxford University Press for 'Out of School' from *Tomorrow is my Love* by Hal Summers.

Lydia Pender for 'Marbles in my Pocket' from *Soundings* published by Holmes McDougall Limited.

Daniel Pettiward for 'Top-secret School'.

The Poetry Society and Book Club Associates for 'Maths Lesson Rules' by Christine Bates and Jill Etheridge; 'Poets' by Elaine Breden; '11 Bus' by S. Hale; 'Profile of a Desk' by J. C. Jeffery; 'Board Rubber' by Gina Staley and 'The Toe Picker' by Debbie Ward, all from *Poets in School*.

Punch Publications Limited for 'Career' by Daniel Pettiward.

Michael Rosen and Penguin Books Limited for 'Rodge Said' and 'Here are the Football Results', part of 'You Tell Me' from *You Tell Me* by Roger McGough and Michael Rosen.

R. C. Scriven for 'The Marrog' and 'Cricketer' from *The Live-long Day* published by BBC Radio for Schools.

Robert Sparrow for 'Dinner Lady', 'Poor Simon Benn' and 'After School'.

Studio Vista for 'From the classroom window' by Neil Bartlett and 'My Teacher' by Kevin Brown from *Poems for Children* edited by Leonard Clark, published in 1970.

Phyllis Telfer for 'The School Bus Breaks Down' by Phyllis Telfer and Hermea Goodman from *Chosen for Children*.

Shirley Toulson for 'Parents Evening' from *Allsorts 4*, published by Macmillan Publishers Limited.

Mrs A. M. Walsh for 'From the Classroom Window' by John Walsh from *The Truants* published by William Heinemann Limited; and for 'I've Got an Apple Ready', 'Bus to School' and 'The Bully Asleep' by John Walsh from *The Roundabout by the Sea,* published by Oxford University Press.

Franklin Watts Limited for 'Banananananananana' and 'Good News' by William Cole from *A Boy Named Mary Jane*.

Jane Whittle for 'The Lollipop Lady', 'In Hall' and 'The Dinner Lady'.

If you're an eager Beaver reader, perhaps you ought to try some more of our exciting titles. They are available in bookshops or they can be ordered directly from us. Just complete the form below and enclose the right amount of money and the books will be sent to you at home.

☐	THE BEAVER BOOK OF MAGIC	Gyles Brandreth	95p
☐	MR ENIGMA'S CODE MYSTERIES	Tim Healy	95p
☐	THE HORROR'S HANDBOOK	Eric Kenneway	£1.00
☐	MORE MAGIC TOYS, TRICKS AND ILLUSIONS	Eric Kenneway	£1.25
☐	CAN PLANTS TALK?	Ralph Levinson	£1.00
☐	HOW TO MAKE SQUARE EGGS	Paul Temple and Ralph Levinson	£1.00
☐	BODY MAGIC	Peter Eldin	£1.00
☐	THE BEAVER BOOK OF TONGUE TWISTERS	Janet Rogers	80p

And if you would like to hear more about Beaver Books, and find out all the latest news, don't forget the Beaver Bulletin. If you just send a stamped-addressed envelope to Beaver Books, 17-21 Conway Street, London W1P 6JD, we will send you the latest one.

If you would like to order books, please send this form, and the money due to:

HAMLYN PAPERBACK CASH SALES, PO BOX 11, FALMOUTH, CORNWALL TR10 9EN.

Send a cheque or postal order, and don't forget to include postage at the following rates: UK: 55p for first book, 22p for second, 14p thereafter; BFPO and Eire: 55p for first book, 22p for second, 14p per copy for next 7 books, 8p per book thereafter; Overseas: £1.00 for first book, 25p thereafter.

NAME..

ADDRESS..

....

Please print clearly